AF217302

Robin Hood

by
David Fermer

Alles Digitale zu diesem Buch kann auf der Lernplattform
allango von Ernst Klett Sprachen abgerufen werden. So geht's:

QR-Code scannen	Buchtitel oder ISBN in	Zum Inhalt navigieren,
oder **www.allango.net**	der Suche eingeben und	direkt abrufen
aufrufen	auf das Buchcover klicken	oder speichern

Dieses Symbol bedeutet, dass zu einem Buch-Abschnitt
ein digitaler Inhalt verfügbar ist.

Ernst Klett Sprachen
Stuttgart

Digitale Extras:
Zu dieser Geschichte gibt es auch das Hörbuch und einen Wortschatztrainer für alle Vokabeln im Glossar. Beides steht dir online zur Verfügung (s. vorherige Seite).

1. Auflage   17 | 2025

Alle Drucke dieser Auflage sind unverändert und können im Unterricht nebeneinander verwendet werden. Die letzte Zahl bezeichnet das Jahr des Druckes. Das Werk und seine Teile sind urheberrechtlich geschützt. Jede Nutzung in anderen als den gesetzlich zugelassenen Fällen bedarf der vorherigen schriftlichen Einwilligung des Verlags.

Autor: David Fermer
Übungen: Heiko Kist
Redaktion: Don Haupt
Layoutkonzeption: Elmar Feuerbach
Umschlaggestaltung: Elmar Feuerbach
Grafik: Matthias Pflügner, Berlin
Tonstudio: custom music, Andreas Nesic, Stuttgart
Sprecher: Paul Newcomb, Stuttgart
Druck und Bindung: Plump Druck & Medien GmbH, Rheinbreitbach

Printed in Germany
ISBN 978-3-12-572261-3

Contents

The characters

The legend of Robin Hood and his Merry Men has been told for centuries and is famous all around the world. Here is a short introduction to the best-loved heroes of the legend – as well as to Robin's enemies!

Robin Hood was famous for taking from the rich and giving to the poor. He was an excellent archer. He lived in Sherwood Forest in Nottinghamshire.

Maid Marian was a Norman noblewoman who fell in love with Robin. Later in the legend, she came to Sherwood Forest to live with Robin.

Will Scarlet was one of Robin's closest friends, also an excellent archer. Some people believe he was once a soldier in the king's army.

The **Sheriff of Nottingham** was Robin's main enemy. He was responsible for capturing outlaws and stopping crime in Sherwood Forest, especially illegal hunting.

Prince John was the younger brother of Richard I, also known as "Richard the Lionheart", King of England in the 12th century. John tried to start a rebellion against Richard while he was away on a crusade.

Friar Tuck was a monk who was expelled from his monastery because of his lack of respect for authority. He was famous for his love of food and wine.

Little John was Robin's second-in-command. He was a giant of a man, over two metres tall. He liked to fight with a long stick called a quarterstaff.

Robin takes his new bow and arrow. He puts the arrow in place and pulls back the string. He closes one eye and aims: a white cross on the wall of his hut. He holds his breath and ...

Robin hears a noise. He turns around and sees something moving in the bushes. A man.

"Please, don't shoot!" the man says as he comes out of the bushes, holding up his hands.

"Who are you?" Robin asks, still aiming at the man.

The man puts his finger to his lips. "Sssshhhh! Not so loud!" he whispers and looks nervously over his shoulder. "The Sheriff's soldiers are looking for me!"

Robin lowers his bow and looks around the clearing. Smoke is coming out of the chimney of his hut. There is no one here but the two of them.

"Please, help me," the man says. "If they find me, they will kill me."

"Come with me," Robin says.

Robin goes over to the well. He pulls the rope and takes out the bucket. "Get in!" he says.

"In there?!" cries the man. His eyes are full of fear.

"Trust me," Robin says.

The man climbs into the bucket and Robin lowers him down into the well.

"You there!" A shout from the forest. Robin turns around. Two soldiers are riding their horses towards him. "Have you seen a man with dark brown hair?" asks one of them.

Robin shakes his head. "I am alone."

"Don't lie to us, farmer!" says the other soldier. "Where is he?"

Robin points to his hut. "I was inside. I only came out to get some water from the well."

"He's not here," says the first soldier. "Let's go back to the road. Maybe we'll find him there."

The two soldiers ride off between the trees. Robin waits for a few minutes, then he calls down the well, "You can come out now!"

"What's your name, stranger?" Robin asks as the two men sit in Robin's hut. Robin gives the man a cup of hot water with herbs.

"My name is Will Scarlet." The man is shaking from the cold water in the well. He holds the cup between his hands and blows the steam into his face. "I am a Saxon from the east."

"What brings you to Sherwood Forest?"

"I was hunting with my brother."

"Where is your brother?"

The man closes his eyes and hangs his head. "He's dead. The soldiers killed him."

Robin puts his hand on Will's shoulder.

"It's not right!" cries Will angrily. He looks into the fire with tears in his eyes. "Sherwood Forest is full of deer! Why aren't we allowed to hunt here?"

"Only the Sheriff of Nottingham and the King of England can hunt here," Robin tells him. "And the king's brother, Prince John."

"While the rest of us go hungry?" says Will. "Where is the justice in that?"

Justice. That was a word Robin hadn't heard for a long time. No one ever spoke of 'justice' in Sherwood Forest. People were too busy trying to survive. When the winter came, many people died from the cold. Life was better in the city. Easier. But many Saxons were not allowed to live there. The Norman rulers didn't allow it.

Robin picks up his new bow and holds it out to Will. "Here. Take this. It's yours," he says to Will.

Will looks at the bow with eyes full of wonder. "Mine?"

"Yes. So that we can hunt together," Robin says.

Will doesn't understand. "But ... I thought hunting was illegal in Sherwood Forest?"

"It is," says Robin with a smile. "So we have to be careful. Very careful."

Robin stops behind a bush and holds his finger to his lips.

"There!" he whispers to Will, who stops beside him. "He's yours."

A deer is eating grass between the trees. Will lifts his bow and looks down his arrow. Suddenly the beautiful animal raises its head and looks straight at the men. Will shoots.

The arrow flies past the deer and hits a tree. The deer turns and runs. Robin already has an arrow ready. He follows the deer with his eye and shoots. Just before the deer disappears behind a tree, the arrow hits it in the neck and the animal falls to the ground.

"Let us take him to the village," says Robin, taking a knife from his belt.

Together Robin and Will carry the dead deer to the next village. The people there are very poor. They eat nothing but soup with beans and corn. For them, the meat of an animal is a luxury.

"This is for you," Robin says as they drop the dead deer next to the village fire. "Everyone in the village should eat from it."

Suddenly they hear a child screaming behind one of the huts.

Robin and Will run to where the cries are coming from. A couple of the Sheriff's soldiers have tied a small boy to the back of one of their horses.

The village people shout at the soldiers. "Leave the boy alone! Let him be!"

One of the soldiers holds up a dead rabbit. "This boy is a thief!" he says. "He stole the Sheriff's property! He's a criminal."

"I didn't steal anything!" protests the boy with the red hair.

The soldier hits him in the face. "We are taking him back to the city for punishment," he says. "He will return in three months. God save the King!"

Then the soldiers ride off, taking the boy with them.

Will looks at the boy's parents. The mother is on her knees, crying.

"They can't just take somebody's child!" says Will angrily.

"Yes, they can," Robin replies, watching the parents. "They can do whatever they want. They will take that boy back to the Sheriff's castle and make him work as a slave. To them, forest children are animals. They can do whatever they want with them."

Robin and Will walk back to Robin's hut. On the way they see some men at the bottom of a hill. "Soldiers!" says Robin. "Let's hide!"

Robin and Will hide behind a bush and watch the soldiers at the bottom of the hill. There are six of them. They are taking off their uniforms and putting on the clothes of poor people, laughing.

Robin and Will move down the hill as quiet as foxes. The men's laughter grows louder. One of them says, "What name shall we give you, captain?"

The captain answers, "What is the name of that farmer who makes the best bows in England?"

"Robin Hood?"

"Yes. Robin Hood. Call me by his name."

Suddenly the soldiers hear something in the distance. They jump behind the bushes at the side of the road.

A small group of riders is coming towards them. Two noblemen and a beautiful woman in a long blue dress. As they pass the bottom of the hill, the soldiers jump out and attack them.

"Give us your money!" they shout, waving their daggers. "Give us your jewellery or we will kill you and feed you to the wolves!"

The two noblemen jump down from their horses and take out their swords, but the soldiers surround them quickly. They don't stand a chance.

"Your ring, m'lady," says the captain. He points to the big golden ring on the lady's finger.

"Who is asking for it?" the lady says.

"Robin Hood," answers the captain.

Suddenly a burning arrow flies through the air and hits the horse's tail. The horse jumps and runs off, carrying the lady away.

"Go to her," Robin tells Will. Will runs down the other side of the hill.

Robin fires an arrow at the man who called himself Robin Hood and calls: "Go before I kill you all!" The arrow hits the man's foot. The man screams and runs off. The other thieving soldiers follow him in panic.

Robin comes down the hill and bows to the noblemen and the beautiful lady.

"I - and nobody else - am Robin Hood!"

Robin and Will walk with the travellers through the forest. The beautiful woman on the horse is called Maid Marian. The two men are her father and brother. She is going to Nottingham because the Sheriff of Nottingham is looking for a wife. Marian's father hopes that the Sheriff will marry his daughter. "I have never met the Sheriff of Nottingham before," says Marian. Robin can hear the sadness in her voice.

They come to a river with a small wooden bridge. The bridge is very thin. Only one man or a horse can cross the bridge at a time. As Robin steps onto the bridge, he sees a man on the other side. The man is as tall as a tree. He has a long stick in his hand.

"Step down from the bridge!" Robin calls to him.

"No, no!" cries the man, laughing. "I was on the bridge first."

"But there are more of us," Robin replies.

"But I am bigger!" says the man. "If you want to cross this bridge, you will have to fight with me."

"Give me a branch," Robin says to Will.

Will breaks a branch off a tree and gives it to Robin. "I will fight with you," Robin says. "The first to fall into the river loses."

Robin and the man fight in the middle of the bridge. Their sticks crack like whips. The man is so strong he almost knocks Robin off the bridge.

Robin moves like an animal. His feet are quick and light. He forces the big man to turn around again and again until the man is dizzy.

"Stay still, you fox!" shouts the man.

But Robin doesn't stand still. He dances around the big man and hits the back of his legs with his stick. The man is so dizzy, he can hardly stand up. Robin pushes him off the bridge.

"You may now cross the bridge, m'lady," Robin tells Maid Marian.

"Thank you, Robin Hood," says Maid Marian.

The big man is splashing around in the water. "You are the great Robin Hood?!" he calls in surprise, spitting out water. "The noble thief of Sherwood Forest who steals from the rich and gives to the poor?" The man laughs. "I was looking for you! My name is Little John. I want to join you!"

"Stealing from the rich and giving to the poor?" Robin says as he cooks a leg of deer over his fire at home. His friends Will and Little John are sitting at the table in his hut.

"You are famous in the city," says Little John.

"But it's not true," Will protests. "Neither Robin nor I steal from the rich. Sometimes we kill a deer and give it to the villagers, but that is all!"

"It is the soldiers who steal from the rich," Robin says. "Today they attacked Maid Marian. They wanted to take her money and jewels."

"And the captain used your name!" Will remembers.

Robin looks into the flames of the fire. "The Sheriff's men have made me an outlaw. If that's what they want, then maybe I will become just that …"

The next day, Robin, Will and Little John go back to the road at the bottom of the hill. They wait in the bushes until a group of travellers comes along the road. Two soldiers and a carriage.

Robin and his men jump out of the bushes. "Hold your horses!" they cry. "This is a robbery!"

Little John pulls the two soldiers off their horses. Will stops the carriage. Robin opens the door. Inside are two young women and a monk.

"Good day, ladies! Are you also on your way to meet the Sheriff of Nottingham?" Robin asks.

The two women look at Robin in surprise. "How do you know?"

Robin takes out a piece of paper. "Please give this to the Sheriff."

The monk takes the note and reads it aloud:

> To the Sheriff of Nottingham: Your soldiers are corrupt. They use my name for their robberies. From today, no road in Sherwood Forest will be safe. Everything I take from its travellers will go to the poor. Robin Hood

The monk looks at Robin. "What a noble cause!" he says and climbs out of the carriage. "I will come with you and protect you with God's word! Good luck with the Sheriff, you horrible women," he says to the young women and hands them the note. "If I were him, I would take neither of you!"

A troop of soldiers rides through the streets of Nottingham. The soldiers are escorting a man with a golden crown.

The soldiers ride quickly, knocking over anything in their way. Mothers grab their children and pull them to safety. On top of the castle walls, a soldier puts a trumpet to his lips and plays a short fanfare.

The gates of Nottingham Castle open. The soldiers escort their prince into the courtyard. A thin man with black and grey hair and a nose like the beak of a bird comes rushing out of the castle.

"Sire!" he cries and falls to his knees as the prince jumps off his horse. "Welcome to Nottingham Castle, Prince John. I hope you had a safe journey."

Prince John waves his hand at the soldiers around him. "Of course I had a safe journey. Not even Robin Hood would attack me, with so many men!"

"You speak the truth." The Sheriff of Nottingham kisses the prince's hand.

"But not everyone has soldiers to protect them," says Prince John. "Things are out of control! You must stop Robin Hood and his band of outlaws!"

Prince John walks into the castle. The Sheriff follows him. "You are right, sire, but how? It is not easy to find Robin Hood in the forest."

"Then you will have to make him come out of the forest!" says the prince.

"But … but how can I do that?" asks the Sheriff.

The Sheriff's soldiers open a door which leads into the Great Hall. Long tables line the room. Men are sitting at the tables. Everyone stands up as the prince enters the room.

"You must give him a reason to come here," says Prince John.

The Sheriff brings the prince to his chair. "But what?"

"There must be something which Robin Hood loves more than the forest," says the prince. He looks up to the balcony which goes all the way around the Great Hall. Many women are sitting on the balcony looking down at the men. One of the women is particularly beautiful. Prince John knows her. Her name is Maid Marian.

"I think I have a good idea," says the prince to himself.

" May the Lord bless this food on our table. Amen!"

The monk called Friar Tuck finishes his prayer as Robin Hood and his men begin their feast in the forest. For many months now, his band of men has been growing. The group is much bigger than it was before. Together they rob Norman noblemen and give the money to the poor.

"It is a wonderful life, is it not?" says Little John, biting into a pig's leg.

"It is," Robin agrees. He watches his men celebrate their latest robbery. They are happy because they are free.

"All we need now are women!" says Will with a romantic look in his eyes.

"Not for me!" Friar Tuck smiles.

Robin looks into the faces of the men around him. Long beards and toothless smiles, dirty faces, knotted hair.

"You are right, Will," Robin says. "It is not good for men to live without women. We must find some women to share our lives with."

"Robin! Robin!" A boy's voice calls from the forest. Robin looks around.

Tom, the red-haired boy who Robin and his men rescued from the city some weeks ago, runs up to the table where Robin is sitting.

"I bring news from the city," the boy says, out of breath. "The Sheriff is putting on an archery competition. The winner will be given a silver arrow as a prize. And guess who will give the silver arrow to the winner?"

Robin looks at the boy and shakes his head. "Tell me."

"Maid Marian!" says the boy. "She's still in the Sheriff's castle."

"Maid Marian?" Robin remembers the beautiful woman in the long blue dress. He remembers the sound of her voice and the touch of her hand.

"You are the best archer in England," the boy says. "You have to take part in the competition, Robin!"

Will jumps to his feet. "No, Robin! You cannot! It's a trap. If the Sheriff catches you, you will never leave the city alive."

Robin looks at Will for a moment, then he says, "Robin Hood is scared of no one."

The streets of Nottingham are full of colour. Flags hang from every house. The town is ready for the biggest event of the year: The Silver Arrow.
The competition takes place outside the walls of Nottingham Castle.
Some men are playing music. Women are dancing. Everyone is happy.
Three men in cloaks and a monk arrive. One of them will take part in the competition. He gives his name to the soldiers. "My name is Roger Godberd," he says. His real name is Robin Hood.
The soldiers write down the man's name and send him over to a target.
"Be careful," Friar Tuck warns him. "The Sheriff's men are everywhere."
Robin takes his longbow and three arrows, and the competition begins. He wins every round. Even the Sheriff, who also takes part, loses against Robin.
"You are a great archer," the Sheriff tells him. "Where do you come from?"
"I come from a small village in the south of England," Robin lies.
The Sheriff doesn't believe him. He tells his soldiers to watch the man who calls himself Roger Godberd. He thinks he is Robin Hood. The Sheriff knows

that Robin will win the competition. And he does. Robin beats every archer in the competition, even the Sheriff's best soldier.

"You are the winner!" says the Sheriff as Robin wins the final. "You will now be given the silver arrow by the beautiful Maid Marian."

Maid Marian steps onto the stage. She gives Robin the silver arrow. When she sees his face, she gasps in surprise. She knows him!

"Stop!" cries the Sheriff. "Tell me, Maid Marian, is it true that you were attacked in Sherwood Forest when you came here a few months ago?"

"Yes, my Lord, I was," answers Maid Marian.

"And was this the man who attacked you?" asks the Sheriff in a voice so loud that everyone can hear him. He points at Robin. "Is this Robin Hood?"

"No! No!" Marian protests. "He didn't attack us. He saved us!"

But the crowd is making so much noise that no one hears her.

"Take him to the dungeon!" shouts the Sheriff.

It is cold in the castle dungeon. Water drips from the ceiling. Rats run across the floor. There is a wooden bucket as a toilet. The food is old and green. There isn't a window in the whole dungeon.

Robin closes his eyes and thinks of Sherwood Forest. Green trees, blue skies, the crystal clear water of the river. Paradise. Nothing could be more different from here.

Robin hears whispering outside his prison cell. The voice of a woman.

"But m'lady!" says a man in reply. "You cannot go in there!"

Again the woman's voice, so soft that Robin cannot hear what she says.

"Very well," answers the man. "But only for two minutes! And don't tell the Sheriff!"

The man brings the woman to Robin's cell. It is Maid Marian.

"What are you doing here?" asks Robin.

"I am here to help you escape," she says, looking over her shoulder to check that no one is listening. "How can I find your men?"

"They have returned to the forest," Robin says. "You could send someone to my hut."

"Where is your hut?"

Robin kneels down. He draws a map in the dirt on the floor. "You must leave the road to York when it crosses the river. Follow the river for a mile, then go south into the forest."

Marian looks at the map and nods.

"You must be careful," Robin warns her. "If the Sheriff finds out you are helping me, he will kill you."

"And he will kill you if we do not help you to escape," Marian says.

Marian puts her hand through the prison bars and touches Robin's cheek. Her hand is warm. Robin kisses her fingers and thanks her.

"Tomorrow night the Sheriff will put on a great feast for Prince John," Marian tells him. "You must be ready for us. We will come during the feast. And once you are free, I will come with you to the forest …"

"We are here for the prince's feast," says Friar Tuck. "We are musicians."
"Musicians?" The soldiers at the gate look at the men from head to toe. They don't look like musicians at all. One of them is the size of a tree!
"The prince is waiting," says Friar Tuck, pointing to the trumpet under his arm. The real musicians are locked up in Robin's hut in the forest.
The soldiers let the men into the castle. They go to the Great Hall. The tables are full of food and wine. People are eating and drinking and singing. Robin's men put their instruments on the stage and go into the kitchen. There they meet with Maid Marian. Marian takes the men down to the dungeon. Three soldiers are guarding the prisoners. Little John attacks them from behind. They tie up the soldiers and take the keys. Marian shows them Robin's cell and they free him.
"So far, so good," says Friar Tuck. "Getting out will be more difficult."
To leave the castle, the men have to go through the Great Hall again. Maid Marian takes them back to the kitchen. She tells the men to wait at the door. She goes out into the Great Hall and starts to sing and dance.

Everyone watches her. Maid Marian is not only beautiful, she also has a beautiful voice and dances like an angel.

While she is singing, Robin and his men quietly go through the Great Hall towards the door. They are just going past the stage when the Sheriff sees them.

"Music!" he calls, clapping his hands. "Music for our beautiful singer!"

He thinks the men are the musicians.

Robin looks at Friar Tuck. Friar Tuck looks at Little John. Little John looks at Will Scarlet. None of them know how to play a musical instrument.

Then the Sheriff sees Robin Hood. "You!!" he shouts, jumping up from the table and grabbing his sword.

"Run!" cries Robin, before the Sheriff can stop him.

Robin's men run out of the Great Hall. They run into the courtyard, but the Sheriff has already sounded the alarm. His soldiers are standing in front of the gates, their swords in their hands.

There is nowhere for Robin and his men to go.

" Put down your swords!" commands the Sheriff.

Robin looks around the courtyard. They are surrounded by soldiers.

He sees some stone steps leading up to the castle wall. Next to the steps the stables are full of horses. Among the soldiers, Robin sees the Sheriff's captain, the man who called himself 'Robin Hood' when he attacked Maid Marian in the forest.

"That is the man who attacked Maid Marian!" says Robin, pointing at the captain. "He is the one who should be in the dungeon, not me!"

The Sheriff looks at his captain and laughs. "Nonsense!"

"It is true!" says Maid Marian. "He and his men dressed as robbers!"

Prince John looks at the captain. His face is red with anger. "Do they speak the truth?"

"I … I …" stammers the captain, but before he can finish his sentence, Robin jumps into the stables and sets free the soldiers' horses. Shouting, he hits the horses and makes them run into the soldiers.

In the tumult Robin and his men run up the stone steps onto the castle wall.
Maid Marian is with them. In the courtyard the Sheriff's soldiers grab their
bows and arrows.

"And now?" asks Friar Tuck. He looks down to the river on the other side of
the wall.

"We jump!" says Robin.

In the courtyard the soldiers are about to shoot.

"Ready?" calls Robin, taking Maid Marian's hand. "One, two, three!"

Robin's friends jump. Robin and Marian follow them. They fall through the air
and land in the water.

"Freedom!" cries Robin.

Yes, freedom and justice. These are the things that Robin Hood lives for.

"Let us go back to Sherwood Forest," he says as he and his men swim to the
side of the river and climb out of the water. He gives Marian his hand and
helps her to her feet. "And you, Maid Marian, will become my wife."

THE END

The times of Robin Hood

The legend of Robin Hood is set at the end of the 12th century, during the reign of King Richard I. Life was very different in the 12th century. Society was organised in what was called a feudal system, which was a kind of pyramid structure, with the king at the top and the poor people at the bottom. People thought that the King of England was chosen by God. The king gave his land to the barons, and in return they gave him money and soldiers. The Church was also very important in the feudal system and owned lots of land, making it more powerful than today.

Life was hard for normal people in the 12th century. They had to pay very high taxes to the landowners. They were not allowed to hunt for animals in the forests. In many ways, the feudal system was similar to slave labour.

There are many theories about where the legend of Robin Hood came from and who the real Robin Hood was. One of the theories is that he was a Saxon soldier who once fought for King Richard. The Saxons came to England from Germany in the 5th century. They were the ruling power until the famous Norman invasion in 1066, when William the Conqueror became the first Norman King of England. After that it was difficult being a Saxon in England. The kings who followed William were also Norman. Most of the barons were Norman. The Normans were rich and the Saxons were poor.

When Richard I became King of England in 1189, he went to fight in the Crusades in the Middle East. While he was away, his younger brother, Prince John, ruled the country. Some people think that Robin Hood also fought in the king's army during the Crusades. When Robin returned to England, he found that the Norman rulers had taken his land. Prince John had raised taxes. When Robin protested, he was declared an outlaw. Whether this version of the story is true or not, it fits perfectly into this time of extremes, and the legend of Robin Hood has come to symbolise the poor people's fight for justice and equality.

The truth behind the legend

The story of Robin Hood is a legend. A legend is a popular story that is not necessarily true or cannot be authenticated historically. The story of Robin Hood is hundreds of years old. In the time before books and television, stories were told when people met around fires or in taverns. Often these stories were sung as ballads. The story of Robin Hood started as an oral story told or sung in such situations. It was first told about a hundred years after the time in which Robin Hood was supposed to have lived.

No one really knows if Robin Hood ever existed at all. He is probably based on a number of different historical figures who did exist in the 12th and 13th century, but whose stories have been mixed up, taking the best from each and changing elements to make it more exciting. No doubt the storytellers' imaginations also played an important role in the creation of the legend.

Two real historical figures, however, might have been the inspiration for the legend of Robin Hood. One of them had a very similar surname: William Robehood. Robehood was an outlaw at the beginning of the 13th century, but he did not live in Sherwood Forest and he didn't steal from the rich and give to the poor. Another outlaw with a very different name, Roger Godberd, had a very similar story to the legend. Roger Godberd lived in Sherwood Forest for four years to avoid being captured by the authorities. The Sheriff of Nottingham at the time was called Reginald de Grey. De Grey captured Roger Godberd and took him to Nottingham Castle, but Godberd escaped. A local knight called Richard Foliot helped Godberd and his friends and protected them from the Sheriff. However, Roger Godberd also didn't steal from the rich to give to the poor. In fact, it is very unlikely that any of the outlaws of the 12th and 13th century were so generous. Life was a constant struggle to survive.

The legend of Robin Hood has been told for hundreds of years, first in ballads, then in books, and later in films. Robin has been many different people, from a former nobleman who lost his land, to a poor farmer who hated the Norman rulers. In many ways, the truth is not important. What remains are the legend's heroic theme and the valour of its hero.

Episode 1

Choose the correct answer.

Robin aims at a man…

A) ☐ with his gun.

B) ☐ with his bow and arrow.

C) ☐ with his knife.

Robin hides the man…

A) ☐ in his hut.

B) ☐ in the bushes.

C) ☐ in the well.

The man says that…

A) ☐ the King´s soldiers are looking for him.

B) ☐ the Queen´s soldiers are looking for him.

C) ☐ the Sheriff´s soldiers are looking for him.

The soldiers arrive…

A) ☐ but cannot find the man.

B) ☐ and arrest the man.

C) ☐ and the man rides off with one of their horses.

Episode 2

Find the words to the pictures.

_____   _____   _____

_____   _____

Episode 3

Read the summary and find the mistakes. Correct the text and copy it into your exercise book.

Robin and Will go hunting. A rabbit is eating grass between the trees. Will shoots and the arrow flies past the animal into the bushes. Then Robin follows the animal with his eyes and shoots. His arrow hits the animal in the head. The two hunters take the animal to the village because the people are poor and they don't have much to eat. The animal is a gift to the villagers. Suddenly they hear a girl screaming behind one of the huts. The Sheriff's soldiers have tied a small girl to the back of one of their horses. The villagers shout at the soldiers. The soldiers say that the girl is a witch.
The soldiers hit the girl on the back of her head and take her to the city for punishment. Her father is crying. Robin says that the soldiers will take the child to the Sheriff's hut and make him work as a cook. To them, forest children are criminals.

Episode 4

Collect important keywords for episode 4 and write them in your exercise book. Try to retell the episode using your notes. Work with your neighbour and practise.

Episode 5

Two new characters appear in this episode.
Write down what you find out about them.

Maid Marian	Little John

Episode 6

Put the questions into the right order and answer them in complete sentences! Check with your partner.

1. is – what – mission – Robin's?
2. does – the – how – help – he – villagers?
3. what – the – do – Sheriff's – do – men?
4. Marian – what – did – the – Maid – Sheriff's – men – do – to?
5. is – outlaw – Robin – why – an?
6. the – following – day – what – do – and – Little John – do – Robin?
7. is – carriage – who – in – the?
8. do – the – where – want – people – to – go – and – why?
9. what – say – the – does – note?
10. the – monk – decide – to – do – what – does?

Episode 7

Read episodes 5–7 again and have a look at the following speech bubbles. Copy the speech bubbles into your exercise book and for each one write who says this and in which situation.

Step down from that bridge!

It is the soldiers who steal from the rich.

You are famous in the city!

I have never met the Sheriff before!

Welcome to Nottingham Castle, Prince John.

You must give him a reason to come here.

What a noble cause!

Crossword

across:
3. without teeth
4. sth you get when you win
5. the Sheriff lives here
6. what a woman wears
7. eine Falle (engl.)

down:
1. grown-up girls
2. a big meal
4. a wish to God
5. a contest

Episode 9

What happens first? Put these sentences into the correct order.

☐ The Sheriff is interested in where Robin comes from. Robin lies to him.

☐ Maid Marian protests and says that this man saved her life, but the crowd is so loud that nobody hears her words.

☐ Roger Godberd is entering the archery competition. The soldiers write down his name.

☐ Robin is thrown into the dungeon.

☐ Maid Marian looks into his face and notices that this man is Robin Hood. She is surprised.

☐ Some men are playing music, women are dancing and everybody is happy and excited.

☐ The Sheriff wants to know if she was attacked in Sherwood Forest by this man.

☐ Robin wins the competition and is given the silver arrow by Maid Marian.

☐ The Sheriff of Nottingham does not believe him at all.

☐ The city of Nottingham is well prepared for the event of the year.

☐ Robin wins every round and even the Sheriff loses against him.

Episode 10

Robin gets help from Maid Marian. She visits him in the dungeon. He tells her the way to his hut in Sherwood Forest. Draw a map of Sherwood Forest and describe the way to his men / hut. These words can help you:

---

leave the road to York when it crosses the river • follow the river for a mile • go south into the forest • enter the forest at... • go left / right at... • go past... • do not go... • don't forget to... • you should... • cross the little stream... • you can see the hut when you... • then you are there!

Episode 11

Match the sentence halves.

The musicians are here	the soldiers are waiting at the gates.
Robin's men	and Little John attacks the guards.
They are allowed into the castle	and sounds the alarm.
She takes them into the dungeon	so that Robin and his men can escape.
They free Robin,	for the prince's feast.
Maid Marian dances in the Great Hall	and meet secretly with Maid Marian.
The Sheriff sees them	but now they have to leave the castle without being seen.
With the swords in their hands	have locked up the real musicians in his hut.

Episode 12

Fill in the gaps with the correct words.

Robin says that the captain is the man who _____ Maid

Marian but the Sheriff thinks this is totally _____. Maid

Marian protests and says that his men were dressed as _____.

Price John turns red in his face with _____. Robin sets free

the Sheriff's _____ and makes them run into the crowd of

_____ .

Answer the questions in complete sentences.

1. Where do Robin and his men run to?
2. How do they finally escape?
3. What are the things that Robin lives for?

Glossary

The characters

introduction Vorstellung
archer ['ɑːtʃə] Bogenschütze
noblewoman Edelfrau
to capture ['kæptʃə] gefangen
nehmen
outlaw Gesetzloser, Bandit
crusade Kreuzzug
friar ['fraɪə] Mönch
monk Mönch
to be expelled ausgeschlossen/
ausgestoßen sein
monastery Kloster
lack of respect Mangel an Respekt
second-in-command stellvertre-
tender Kommandeur
quarterstaff Kampfstab

Episode 1

bow [bəʊ] Bogen
arrow Pfeil
to put in place platzieren
to pull back zurückziehen
string hier: Bogensehne
to aim zielen
hut [hʌt] Hütte
to hold one's breath die Luft
anhalten
to turn around sich umdrehen
to be looking for sb jdn suchen
to lower hier: senken
clearing Lichtung
well Brunnen
rope Seil
to climb klettern

to shake one's head den Kopf
schütteln
to lie (lied, lied) lügen
to point to sth auf etwas zeigen
to ride off davon reiten

Episode 2

stranger ['streɪndʒə] Fremder
herbs [hɜːbz] Käuter
to shake (shook, shook) hier:
zittern
to blow (blew, blown) blasen,
pusten
steam Dampf
to hunt jagen
angrily verärgert, wütend
tear Träne
deer Hirsch
to go hungry hungern
justice ['dʒʌstɪs] Gerechtigkeit
busy beschäftigt
to survive überleben
ruler Herrscher
to pick up aufheben
illegal ungesetzlich

Episode 3

to raise [reɪz] anheben, hochheben
straight geradeaus, hier: direkt
to disappear verschwinden
nothing but nichts als
corn Getreide
to drop fallen lassen
to scream schreien, heulen
tied gebunden

to leave sb alone jdn in Ruhe lassen
Let him be! Lass ihn in Ruhe!
property Eigentum
punishment Bestrafung
to reply antworten, erwidern
slave Sklave

Episode 4

to hide sich verstecken
in the distance in der Ferne
noblemen Edelmänner
dagger Dolch
jewellery [ˈdʒuːəlri] Schmuck
to feed *hier:* verfüttern
to surround sb jdn einkreisen,
  umstellen
thieving diebisch
to bow [baʊ] sich verbeugen

Episode 5

sadness Traurigkeit
wooden hölzern, aus Holz
stick Stock
branch [brɑːntʃ] Ast
crack *hier:* knallen
whip Peitsche
to knock sb off *hier:* hinunterstoßen
to force jdn zwingen
dizzy schwindlig
to splash herumplanschen
to join sich jdm anschließen

Episode 6

neither ... nor weder ... noch
villager Dorfbewohner

carriage [ˈkærɪdʒ] Kutsche
robbery Raubüberfall
corrupt [kəˈrʌpt] korrupt,
  bestechlich
safe sicher
noble cause noble Sache
to protect (be)schützen
to hand sb sth jdm etwas geben

Episode 7

to escort eskortieren, begleiten
to knock over umstoßen
to grab schnappen, packen
courtyard [ˈkɔːtjɑːd] Innenhof
beak [biːk] Schnabel
to rush eilen, rennen
Sire *hier:* Majestät
to lead into sth (led, led) zu etwas
  führen
to line *hier:* aufgereiht sein
to enter hineingehen
reason Grund
particularly besonders

Episode 8

feast [fiːst] Festessen
knotted [ˈnɒtɪd] verknotet
to rescue retten, befreien
to put on veranstalten
archery competition Bogen-
  schießwettbewerb
trap Falle
to be scared Angst haben

Glossary

Episode 9

event Ereignis
to take place stattfinden
cloak [kləʊk] Umhang
target Ziel
she gasps in surprise [gɑːsps] ihr
  bleibt vor Schreck die Luft weg
to point at sb auf jdn zeigen
dungeon [ˈdʌndʒn] Verlies, Kerker

Episode 10

to drip tropfen
ceiling [ˈsiːlɪŋ] (Zimmer)Decke
prison cell Gefängniszelle
to escape fliehen, entkommen
dirt [dɜːt] Schmutz, Dreck
to nod (mit dem Kopf) nicken

Episode 11

musician [mjuːˈzɪʃn] Musiker
gate Tor
from head to toe von Kopf bis Fuß
to be locked up eingesperrt sein
stage Bühne
to guard [gɑːd] bewachen
prisoner Gefangener
to sound the alarm den Alarm
  auslösen

Episode 12

to lead up hinaufführen
stable [ˈsteɪbl] Stall
among unter, zwischen
to speak the truth die Wahrheit
  sagen

to stammer stottern
to set free freilassen
tumult Verwirrung, Tumult

Additional information

reign [reɪn] Herrschaft
in return als Gegenleistung
tax Steuer
similar ähnlich
slave labour Sklavenarbeit
he was declared an outlaw er
wurde
  zum Gesetzlosen erklärt
to fit passen
equality Gleichberechtigung

to authenticate [ɔːˈθentɪkeɪt] *hier:*
  bestätigen
tavern Schänke, Gastwirtschaft
oral mündlich
to be based on basieren auf
doubt [daʊt] Zweifel
local hiesig, ortsansässig
generous [ˈdʒenrəs] großzügig
a constant struggle to survive ein
  ständiger Kampf ums Überleben
nobleman Edelmann
valour [ˈvælə] Wagemut